No Map of the Earth Includes Stars

No Map of the Earth Includes Stars

Christina Olivares

Marsh Hawk Press

East Rockaway, NY · 2015

15 16 17 18 19 7 6 5 4 3 2 1 First Edition

Marsh Hawk Press books are published by Poetry Mailing List, Inc.,
a not-for-profit corporation under section 501 (c) 3
United States Internal Revenue Code.

Cover photo, *Panoramic of Medina,* by Christina Olivares.
Cover and interior design by Claudia Carlson. Author photo is a self-portrait.
The text is set in Garamond Premier Pro and titles in Adobe Jenson Pro.

Library of Congress Cataloging-in-Publication Data

Olivares, Christina.
   [Poems. Selections]
   No map of the Earth includes stars / Christina Olivares.
      pages cm
   ISBN 978-0-9906669-0-5 (pbk.) -- ISBN 0-9906669-0-5 (pbk.)
   I. Title.
   PS3615.L55A6 2015
   811'.6--dc23

                           2014035356

Marsh Hawk Press
P.O. Box 206
East Rockaway, NY 11518-0206
www.marshhawkpress.org

for my family

for L.R., who is love

for all of you, of and not of this world, searching,
and naming your living, and loving

&

in honor of Arturo and José

may these words be yours in the sea

Contents

PETITION

Burnt Code

Scans show progress in the left temporal lobe. Denial of illness. Disordered thoughts, made-up words. System central to your nervous. I hold your dis-ease, a handful of burnt threads. Threads made of sea. Hands made of making sense of. And there was a flight, remember? Child-you crossing and during the crossing splitting into a jangling that could not corroborate its own song—

tongued water tangled into a dividing mind. Those angels? A drowned chorus. Straining to be heard by you. Light fracturing, split-open light only you can see and hear. Coded words, messages abbreviated. A series of intuitive experiences leave you certain you are chosen by God, and some god-part of you is consoled. Relieved. But God's a tease. Your inner light is by turn mild then frightening, a burst filament.

Divinity made you a temporary prophet, lit you on fire, filled your mouth with the mouths of the crossed sea, the sea filled with voices, till you floated on signs. See? Hardwired you for listening. Then abandoned you to your fear. You devote years to listening to, interpreting, misinterpreting code. Origin: intuition. Or an adverse post-migration experience. Or centuries of such. Origin: beautiful song, weightless in your ears as you grip a train pole. The dead sing to us, and sometimes, reluctantly, we hear. Rarely do we listen. You do, but—

the police take you and take you and take you. Cloth in your mouth, cloth for teeth, what is wrong, you ask me, *did they cut your tongue out, daughter? When you sent me into this place?* I shake my head, silent as slit cords. White waxy floors. Your fat, pill-studded eyes, vacant hands. Scans insist a progression. You are my body of memory. The strings that bound you to what was are cut but they trail you, wet and adrift. Dislocated, melting pot. I stir ash with a fingertip, hold your burnt code to the light.

Palimpsest

Palimpsest sediment was deposited under one set of environmental conditions, then strongly influenced by another set of conditions, so that sediment has lost properties imparted by the original agent of deposition:

flight over water, night flight. Studies show there is no smooth sailing. City beckoned. To be come a new home. Disordered thoughts, made-up words. How could he hurt anyone, officer? He is naked. Arrested in hallucinating flight:

statistically probable for you to develop this seeing. Religious and paranoid. Immigrant: memory re- and dis-membered. Reality laid over reality until nothing is whole any longer. Always new.

Exile

Crisis: when the kidnapped crossed the sea, new names were assigned to old spirits. Saint Lazarus is Babalu Aye. Covered in boils, odious and leaking, Babalu Aye is exiled to a forest. In exile, he cultivates a new seeing. Prophet, deity, god, orisa. His new seeing heals him. Society, which once rejected him, now worships him. His presence, once the catalyst for epidemic, is an innoculation. Suffering is contagious: we catch it, like fear, from one another, mostly without noting the source. Now people journey miles to be blessed at his church in Rincón. Papa, is this your story? No. Exile is the opposite of sea: four white, memoryless walls, containing you against your will. No new respect was accorded your skin. At Rincón, I lay flowers, scrape the trough of warm colored wax and light purple candles. Babalu Aye is mine, conferred by the young drunken santeros is a Havana house of spirits one savagely hot summer. *Hecho de palabras*. A healer orisa invoked by many tongues, *lenguas*. Some lost. Some reinvented. Birth, the inevitable result of telling. I have found these wet scraps of tongue for you, Papa, at the bottom of the sea we are. Listen:

Childhood

When the engine spits and thrusts on,
you, Papa, clench your face,

or you are asleep, lips slack on your mother's arm, the sea beneath you:

night flight, stars
above a widening sea.

> *I saw that the world is coded, constellations,*
> *and I am a key that opens stars, I see infinite too.*

Sea unfurls her kinks high
over the Malecón, you are eight, crossing overhead.

> *Saw the earth and sea are full of holes to fall through, and falling,*
> *become, far above the sharp angels calling up to me.*

Trembling but too old to be carried to the new home when you land,
new land, snow rises your eyes,

stars in your mouth
become grains of snow.

Melting pot: other children throw chairs, you get fluent in their tongue. Your father, tipsy, reels out of the frame. City, no pigs to slaughter. Your mother a holy entity, holding up the apartment with one hand, dusting the blessed conch in the dining room with the other, its white ridges pressed into a hymn. Saints line her dresser. Don't touch the prayers whirling below their feet: a floor built of disintegrating words. Small room to yourself under a hammered tin ceiling. Work in the bakery, your thin brown arms sloughed in wet sugar, nurse unsteady kittens in your bathrobe pocket. Begin to suspect you are born to decode what others can't. A strangeness comes over you sometimes. Quell the voices licking at your eardrums in stiff waves with sex, sleep, drawings, drugs. Pot too cold, nobody melts.

Illness as a mirror: the first time you saw an alien. Or a group of aliens hovering: a lit dandelion fluff over Harlem. You say *Brighter than anything I'd ever seen.* During a storm, a storm-lit sky, your body framed in the kitchen window. Bedroom window? The telling and retelling fuck up the details: palimpsest. You say *A lovely halo.* After initial encounter you saw the light and intuited the source of the light shrouding an alien figure in the window. Unlike yet bright as stars. A sign of things to come. You call your sisters to the window: they see but deny, or don't come. Or you never call them.

Your mother's memory: after the revolution, never enough milk to soothe your cries. One bus runs an illegal night route to a farm, under stars and moon slung low in a cooling sky. She risks it every week. Risks it all, pays a little, so you are consoled.

You, learning to work in the bakery: floured floor, kittens underfoot, cartoon characters cut out and taped to the wall, sugary tavern of the innocents. Decorate cakes, cut thinnest pastries, carry the heavy batter, suffer the heat. Ovens wider than a child's wingspan. Rusted and caged fan above the back door. Your sweat, your salt, your naked hands plunged in dough, then in water, then in dough again. Sugar a filth that clings and suffuses. Barrels of sugar, barrels of flour. Wisps of gold foil, silver dots the trembling size and color of spilt mercury. Freeze then slice cake, drop teaspoonfuls of cookie on the burnt baking sheets. You adapt to routine. No wasted movements: execution as deliberate as a canecutter. Exhaustion. Agitation stirs in you, difficult to name. You surrender your thinking mind to the thoughtless rhythm of chemistry, to rules that cannot, no matter how much the world tries, be undone.

You Hear Singing on the El Train

onset of what
the doctors call paranoid
schizophrenia is here
signaled by a strong
positive delusion of
religious grandeur
particularly
a calling to messianic
duty—

when it happens it happens SUDDENLY.

like: a first shock of recognition—this is love—I am in love—I am love, I am in love.

or

like: flying airborne, realizing it's only dream—maybe a lucid dream—you can control it— and all is real and not-real, chosen and not-chosen—and the act of waking up wipes your mind mostly clean, dream's phantom limb still ascending.

or

like: you have sustained some serious injury—the delay between the knife in flesh and the pain receptors that begin clamoring, then exploding. like:

a crash of *suddenness. And then there was—*

LIGHT sputters through bridge beams, everything
sings, synesthesia and angels

unfolding from your damp
palms, you bend your head and curl your lips over the snatches
you hear

auditory hallucination

look at the ruined people—beautiful—
all around you—dumb and closed and incohate—

listen to the singing—frantic wing-beating, a heart-
beat, you are dissolved in the new sunlight, it is shards of angels,
each springing up around you in pools, singing—

what you thought you knew, you can't remember
what you want to know, you mouth to yourself viciously, blessed,

close your eyes you are so sure   so sure this is true

it is

you are arrested
by the radiance of every single thing
on this train   every single   thing

you'll be called to save them

this knowing you contain
you are a brimmed vase filled with light
a brimmed light of veins and snow   the skin you are begins to sing

for the first time
as if god—casual as morning coffee—
on the train into work   stripped a mortal filter
from your skin, and you

KNOW you are chosen
you always knew that beneath your skin lived a messenger
god would recognize and claim

don't we all
want this
deep down:
our prodigal
selves
to be blessed
wholly
in a way
we cannot even fathom
blessing ourselves

to mimic
your shaking breath   your dilated heart
your hands made of unyielding road and flight

the train

rocks

knowingly

when it happens it happens suddenly, all studies show

everything is you

everything is a mirror; hold it up
and see the daughter in the corner
holding it up; see yourself beside her;

everything is

everything
is you:

the train, the angel-song, the too-bright light,
the half-awake riders, the
children at home, the wife, the broken-toothed city—

but even as you pulse—sublime,
limitless, shadowless, inconquerable,

the *light* shifts, the el train linoleum
appears more stained, every human sound around you
becomes obscured,
a haunting enters, some old melody in a minor
key replaces the angels, the chords
jangle, the song stops—

when intuition gives way
when god leaves you only
memory of one
glorious train ride—

you, annointed
and directionless—when
god stops singing and starts to whisper—when you are left
with the failed love, the woken-dream,
the knife set deep in flesh, and nerves begin to talk—

then the search for you, Papa,
begins:

as soon as your knowing listening begins

the train rocks

knowingly   pitched into a wide Bronx sky

you grasp at the fading bright thing—the fading song—mocking
you now—you are changed forever—you know what the saints knew
all of it;

the impression of knowing stays; any actual knowing
leaves; a reckless angel left a footprint in your mind

what do daughters know?

A man asks you directions, you can't
hear him—you say—*WHAT*—

Incomplete List of First Rank Symptoms

in which voices assimilate translate transmit voice one's thoughts aloud

in which two voices spit operatic for one's bliss/blues

in which the voices recast illumine foreshadow

in which one's mind is while sleeping is opened by ill-behaving sourceless hands

in which every single event is a syllable in a code

delusions of intuition: certainty that one is chosen

delusions of intuition: certainty one's seeing is correct and can be trusted

Sea Claims the Temporary Prophet

Your deep and constant alarm: background noise turned all the way up, lurid as colors clamoring for you. Sound brighter, heavier, wrong. No distraction suffices. Impaired empathy. Self-centered. Self as center. The world is a mirror opening in infinite directions. Or the world is two mirrors facing each other, you standing between them, you knowing that just as the infinite reflection curves out of view, just out of your reach, *that is where God is*. You are convinced some god *is*. But. You are in the way. Shake your head rhythmically side-to-side to clear out the excess thoughts. You're chosen. And not ill: the world is ill and stalking you. Haphazard angels scurry through your mind, leaving behind imprints of their presences. Incomprehensible beauty. Negative symptoms: blunting of affect. Exquisite and frightening present. Voices running commentary on your every action, nerve impulse, thought. Quick to anger, fearful. You don't care about the exact nature of reality. You are more concerned about this: when you touch the white walls designed to contain you, sometimes they dissolve into your hands.

Everything is
reparable except
what is not done
breaking

Studies show that paranoid and religious phenomenology in schizophrenic clinical presentation is substantially increased in Afro-Caribbean male immigrant population reasons unknown. Studies show that mode of onset and symptom profiles of psychoses suggest that atypical syndroms and by implication misdiagnoses do not account for reported higher rates of schizophrenic illness in these patients. Studies show that in particular auditory hallucinations and certain first rank symptoms have assumed diagnostic significance in certain cultures may not necessarily have the same significance in certain Other cultures.

Star dust—
you dissolve
statistics
with tap
water, smuggle
them down
the drain,
hide them
under your
tongue, spit
them quickly
into half-
eaten dinner,
crush them
into a powder
in your pocket
and push a
small cloud
out
a little
hole—

Sea is the instigating witness—hands, hacked history, eyes, many-mouthed, the stars above, altering—she claimed you—she fundamentally uprooted your perception—what was left, an absence of what you know, the cords of snapped roots, still soft, wormy, a dank, perfect smell, full of life, diminishing by the second—still the rich earth is stilled—this is called seeing, or insanity—sea's girth—remind how strange perception becomes and becomes again—who she contains—the dead-living mouths within, a haunting reaching to fill any listening ear—You say,

I see, I see. You can't see what I see—

That's true, Papa—but I can hear—

You can't hear what I hear.

Mind unfolds
expands
falls away, a star

A sea
taken root
explodes from your skull
wet splitting

was from *is.*

You stand
inside those white walls, swaying.

I know things you can't see.
They came before me. They'll come again
after I'm gone.

You say delusion *but I'm not delusional.*

You say delusion *and will drug me until*
this thing inside of me you're frightened of
is dead but my skin itself is what is made

of memory that comes. Comes and stays.

Positive predictors of outcome: positive, not negative (lacking) symptoms. Presence of normal emotions. Good initial response to medication. Paranoia.

A strand of exhaust: a cloudless blue blue. A thin line dividing *was* from *is*. Almost all cases involve delusions of religious grandeur and governmental persecution.

Unsolveable mystery: illness of the mind. No innoculation. Best to keep the patient comfortable until he is reasonable again.

Dictation: Papa Medicated with Thorazine

Dictation: Papa When Served Chili

I will
not eat
any chili
that you
put bodies
in
their snapped
brains stick
to my rib
oyster-slick
and water rotted
you're sick
they tongue
your gut
fuse hips joints
collarbone
skull with yours
you will
become
a dead thing
like them
behind your teeth
strings of
saliva mash
these thistlebreathed

voiceless
your tongue
corrupted
your will
co-opted
silly child
foolish
little stupid
fucking girl
there are
people
in your mouth
let them
out

Allocution

meaning draws into the ordinary

                                          narrow field of stars

does rupture in the mind
reflect rupture in the spirit

ordinary turns bright
through your narrow veins

does rapture in the mind destroy
or preserve the remembered self

two or more voices arguing

                                              body

one or many voices commenting on one's actions

                                                sea

certainty that what the doctor calls delusion is reality

                                          constellation

the purposes served by rapture
by our rupture

I touch your hot forehead

Does rupture serve a purpose beside allocution of or avoidance of pain—

Does the spirit exist,
does the mind.

Childhood

Age little: you paint my face a smiling payasita, and we mimic war for Titi's camera, her costume jewelry adorning my tiny rag-fitted body. Tickle wars. To make me eat dinner, you put bits of American cheese between my freshly-bathed toes. I say I will marry someone just like Papa. Your love is specific, directive. When you teach me to defend myself, I break noses. *If they bleed, they'll quit. Their fear is your best defense.*

You lifted my palm to rest on your sweat-filthy forehead. My fingers contracted: I climbed off the bunk and went to the bathroom to wash my hand when you walked away.

Christmas: cousins racing between rooms. I'd dragged my fingers along the chicken's warm-boned carcass, still-warm grease, salt. Touched the tree lights to see when the dull warmth would flood into shock-pain, how hot things make sudden surprise in the nerves.

No pain. But you were absent. The feeling in my belly, a herd of small discomfort. You were missing. Then I felt you return, apartment caving around the space you had emptied,

then filled again, inversion, key turning, voices. You were sweat-filthy and it was sticky on your forehead like chicken grease. You were full of lies as you were shifting into a new being, except it was true when you stole my palm-map to say, *Heal me.* But I didn't.

My teeth are brined in apocalypse Oreos. My milky-mouthed brother squishes fingers into his glass, excavating a melting treasure. It's your job to notice, but you've relinquished the difficulty of seeing us. Your eyes travel up, north, heaven, new dictums dropping while I see bombs gliding lazy and haloed over the East River, just in time to prove you right.

Keep sitting here. Eat your cookies. See the sun curling over clouds? Imagine a giant explosion. Evil people will die, all of them. For us, my children, it's heaven. We'll watch this world become a whole new world. A light will tear open the sky, swallow us. We are already torn and swallowed. Watch this, watch how quickly we disappear.

You explain on our rural walk—my mother is hiding in our friend's basement, February memory says the spare leaves are yellow, clotted brightly in a hovering sunlight, this is wrong, it was cloudy—*This is what you're born to do.* In the distance, something on fire. *Are you listening?* Last night you put your hand in the fireplace to prove the new voices in you. The beauty that is not yet dead in you will soon be torched by lithium, foreign hands. Because I am your perfect girl, I divide my heart in half and offer half to your devouring thing. Yes Papa, you can trust me. I promise. I cut my throat, offer the cords for burning. It's cold, ash-cloudy, you and I are far from anywhere, we are moving between cities, literally, our home is ash behind us, literally—small map that fit between my tracing fingers, child's palmful of distance.

Explaining you to the guidance counselor: What we call hallucinations, a small way of discrediting another's seeing. Your terror is a neurochemical process involving prescription thorazine, crossing, loud angels, absence of the above, and genetic predisposition. Your terror is not what you would call terror but *revelation, observation, insight, hilarity.* Your terror is visual, auditory, oblique, synesthetic. *Fear is what makes us human and the same. Anything not afraid is not animal. If it isn't animal, it's here to destroy me.* I stopped fearing you; you took exigent action.

The police come but they don't come unmarked, without sirens, how I asked when I called them, barefoot with my brother in tow. You are naked in your skin, your hands empty, refusing to put clothes on, when they pull out handcuffs. *I'll kill everybody in the house if you call the police.* When I see fear spasm in you, my own spooled breath eases. *Pigs are demons.* You and I, our threads rip past the seam. *Beat and spat on me.* But you pulled a knife on her, so I win: court-mandated hospital stay, the first of a handful of spaces of relief. Upon release, you inspect the food I serve. I see your signs, I learn your signs, hunted girl.

Statistically you are not even interesting, you are predictable, you are predicted. And predictable as you are, you also predict correctly: everything is destroyed. You, code-breaker. Us, the sky you light on fire. It isn't your fault. It was the singing in you, you couldn't possibly contain it.

Exigence: Divide her. After eviction, new rental, put her on the first floor. Move self, wife, other child into the tiny upstairs. Peer through the crack in the door while she sleeps. Tell her she is a spy. Destroy her things. Drive erratically, accident as goal. Wander into her room in the middle of the night, strip off your clothes, peel skin back. Stand naked as stars in the window, body as warning. Shower in the bathroom attached to her room. If one night, under advisement from a guidance counselor, she locks her bedroom door, scream and bang until she opens. Explain nothing. In daylight, graze your hand against her softest parts: harden her. She will harden.

On rare visits home I tuck a kitchen knife under my pillow, sleep fingering the handle. College a series of small things, none as terrifying as you. I find the mouths of your sea familiar, relevant: Cuba on a school trip. Promise myself I'll be a revolutionary, an oracle, transcendent, a poet, all my own. When the gyn parts my hips during that last summer, I flinch. There are no blood-smeared dream walls here, just the echo of things that should never have been, and won't be quieted.

Why I Went

The sea is a body that holds
all of what we were forced to
unbecome. Hidden in her
mouths, a wept, wild singing.

The Malecón is a spine binding
fragile colonized earth to the sea.
Her mouths open to tear
granite from between my legs.

I dangle my legs. If I dropped
my shoes, one would land in the sea.
The other would land on the earth.
I visited your uncle Arturo today.

My great uncle Arturo hides his
machete in the stove with no
mouth. He sees how you see,
Papa, deciphering codes from nothing.

Papa, Arturo sold the house
down to the bone, lithograph of his
mother pasted to the wall, gone
iron, glass, floor tiling. A flood of

tiny roaches. Arturo, Papa is like you,
Papa, Arturo is like you, but I am
liminal, a girl perched on the spine
of a haunted thing I can't name or ride.

Let me speak sense to you: the bones of that house
are softer than you would imagine, eroded
by his insanity, which is not love, and you
were a boy there, I felt you there,

as a boy. Still chained to your earth
and not yet chasmed by grief. Before the sea
claimed you as her own. Before me.
Let it break your heart instead of mine.

House of Spirits

Mess of flies and offering-stink in the cramped backyard, animals stacked in cages until sacrifice. Near the babalawo's blue room, inscribed walls, sharp hunger of meat frying. Laughter and a child barreling through the house, bellowing at full power. Reused bottles of aguardiente and braided bead necklaces and knives and figurines and feathers and books. A corner stained in a lone thin red streak, floor to ceiling. At some point they mashed coconut and put it against our heads. And we stood in circles of sunlight, quietly. I drank from a small Dixie cup filled with—I was blindfolded, it tasted of warmed tears. Somebody wept and it pulled strings in our bodies—an old quiet thing. Hidden in our mouths, a wild singing—this:

Babalu Aye? they ask. Babalu Aye, I respond. Affirm. No, not him, they say. Yes, him, I insist. It is him. Too rare and hard. Ask for another one. Ask for Yemaya, you seem to be kin to the sea. Ask for Ochun, you are also beautiful. I shake my head no. We drink together first. The youngest one's face becomes serious as he slaps palm nuts against the cracked floor. Yes, he sighs. Babalu Aye. The others crowd to look. I knew all along, Papa. I knew he was mine. Why else would he have given me you.

Kneel on the blood and honey wet tiling. Rum so highly proofed it numbs my mouth. Here is where the atrocities come to rest. Grip his fingers, Papa, the old leper is waiting for you at the edge of the forest. Edge of the known. Go in. Some part of the sea become a rain to wash you clean. Leave me the salt, leave me your eyes. Go in.

Petitioning Babalu Aye

You were a map of stars, drawn all over again.
You a field of the invisible. Things would be drawn into you.

The cold peeled your stubborn skin,
but skin did not melt as instructed:

because it never melted this was not your home.

In flight you saw something freewheeling
above within and below you that you could not name.

The sea claimed you, this is indisputable, but here is
the permanent mystery: wild mind, root of sea,

why your new seeing? How did reality replace reality?

Illness as palimpsest. Illness that is not in and of itself illness,

just one mind's reaction to a new world, new language,
same way a body makes fever to fight an infection,

same way a spirit will come down during ceremony—

People prepare
their whole lives
to be the right
vessel into which
an orisa pours
himself. Others
write themselves
into being. I witness
the dancer
take on Babalu
Aye in un centro
comunitario:

the dancer sings as if his mouth is a net in the sea blossoming his
wrist twists grotesque the rest of him follows—jerky bent thing
made of hinges somebody hands him stumbling a crutch a splintered
bit his tongue juts out a body no longer in mastery of itself his
tongue juts out blindly seeking to lick any open wound any of our open
wounds someone spills water on the ground I want to wet your forehead
back of neck throat induce a miracle

his tongue would first mash your eyelids kiss the seeing place first

He bears a resemblance   to you
as an old man, Papa: skin wrinkled
hair   the color of varnished teeth

your skin, his skin   placeless as the salt in the sea

he a king, you a myth

our witness
keeps gods
and fathers
alive

he bears a resemblance   to you, Papa
reimagined

a man in a broken body
a body filled with god, translated:

mud figure melting in salt-

scarred rain. Built of tongues.

Built him new in a new place,

gave him a new name, concealed

his features in a new face. And you:

down or avoid the pill. I petition

for you, Papa, for him to lay on

your thrumming broken mind.

There is no satisfying or accounting for the daughter's desire to see with the father's unseeing eyes. Prepare the altar. Choose the quietest water, image of San Lazaro, square of burlap, bowl of milk. Flower: stay there until fear washes me clean of fear.

Lay the photo of the men cutting sugarcane on the altar. Is everything the way it needs to be—how do I make an avenue for Babalu Aye's foot to come wandering down here. For you, for me. *I am ruined.* How does he choose which pain to attend to. How much needs to be sacrificed in order to hear clearly. Where exactly does he come rushing into, anyway: pore, spine, glass of cooled milk? As if without violence he couldn't enter at all.

History is entirely violence—actual or imagined. And it is a girl, sitting in a sugarcane field, ripping sheets of paper and letting the wind take them, one by one, two by two, while the men cut, delicate muscle and machete under a ruby blister of sun. You were a baker before you were touched and the sea started clamoring in you. Your hands are made for sugar. Mine, for listening.

Grip the cushion, watch the sea, impassive, fall beneath. Her persistent tongues. Her tremendous amalgamation of body. But not even a whisper fled from her throat to mine. I imagine the dead are exhausted by our refusal to live, to say the story straight, as they push eons of unspoken against our recalcitrant mouths. For us to do the small courtesy of naming, therefore seeing. But what is there left to be afraid of? Everything's happened to us already. What happens again is only echo.

Rincón (Babalu Aye Responds)

Rutted interior road. Church breathes a damp salt although we are miles inland. Twice a day a man scrapes the troughs of melted dark wax, candles burnt past wick. Colors tumble, stark and bled mellow. He hands me the trowel. I scrape. For the memory of my hands moving through the carcasses of others' prayers. In case there is nothing else. We circle the ceiba out back, setting on our tongues an alive prayer. Earlier, I bit the center of a flower that burnt sweet on my tongue—my tongue—while the laden donkey farted and kicked up blinding clouds of dust, memory—and later when I am tucked into a friend's bed in Centro Havana, a song rises inside me, from the same intuition that destroyed you: *Hear for me inside the ruined bodies, even your father's, for the seeing place inside each one of us that is not blind with fear. Listen:*

Glossary

aguardiente — highly proofed rum used in religious ceremonies

babalawo — priest in the Ifá tradition of Santería

un centro comunitario — a community center

lenguas — may be translated as either tongues (anatomical) or languages

hecho de palabras — made or built of words

el Malecón — the vast concrete sea wall, built under Spanish rule, edging most of Cuba's northern (Caribbean) coastline

orisa — spirit or deity that reflects a manifestation of divinity in Santería

payasita — dimininutive and female form of *payaso*, which means *clown*. *Payasita* translates as *little girl clown*.

Santería — a pantheistic religion originating in Yoruban culture, adapted and synchretized somewhat with Catholicism; this book deals specifically with Santería as it exists within Cuba and throughout the Cuban diaspora.

santeros — priests in Santería

OTHER LIVES

Sunday Morning: Ars Poetica

Outside the Latin grocery, two crates full
of mangoes in the shape of plump commas, the size
of children's palms. Yellow-hued,
brown-freckled, here and there streaks of green,
an uncommon flush of rose. Deep within my own
tendons some other fruit swells and aches,

heavy as an unsung song—tonight it'll burst,
yield a clotted dark honey, a thin
red rain on my shorts. Curled beside me, you'll
press both hands on the razored skin
below my belly where a child could be.
I've started to love the body's thunderstorm,

drug it less. Limit what I feel and I'll quickly forget
limitlessness, our shared need to be
generous or close. I choose six,
three in each hand. My cycle begins to set
teeth on the inside of my abdomen. I remember
standing on the beach in Cuba once with a girl,

peeling their small ripe skins back with our mouths,
sucking the pulp then the threads from
each other's tongues, clear down to the pit,
then throwing the pits and skins into the bright
sea & diving in afterwards. *There must be groves
of mango trees down there*, she said. Imagine

the warm salted dark, silvered by fish nibbling their new
treasure—first unaccustomed, then expert,

their tiny fins seeking, while mangoes
float on firm stems, a cloud of planets. That day I'd fled
from language, swimming like a fool
till each limb went slack—I floated, I was just an eyelash

on the turning waves, curious about drowning—
can we say the beauty that comes into us after we go,
before we leave our lives? Everything said, finally, nothing wasted, like
a finished bloom bedded into and becoming soil, a loosening blood rinsing
me clean. It's just a dollar for all six, heft of liquid sweet:
two for me, two for you, & two for the ones who like small things.

Visiting Your Father

The national cemetery sits on Honolulu the way a brain sits on top of a body,
diagrammed into lobes, or lungs—the air is clear, exquisite, diamonds in the mouth.

Imagine, Mama: in a suspended city of foreign, restless dead, a tattooed man rides a
lawnmower over cut and cut grass. Thick scent rises like just before rain.

Avoid the northern shore during storms, when the undercurrent blossoms to
drown. Avoid likewise the mirror of earth: *perhaps his killing is in me.*

Section A, Site 324-C. You believe in honor, in white wars. He left you, did not come
back for you, laying your head on the grass beside the small white cross.

Call him, the way a poem calls you. Say, *parent, I am here. I am here.*

Kigali Journals, 2006

A woman asks my friend and I if we are saved. This woman is the receptionist at the church compound where we live these weeks in Kigali. Shy of her question, we tiptoe around the answer. She invites us into her room, makes us coffee. We begin a spontaneous language instruction. She teaches us words in Kinyarwanda, my friend teaches us those same words in Yoruba and I translate into Spanish. *Bread, coffee, earth, love, fucking.* I ask for a French lesson and the woman gently refuses, wondering if there is a language in Cuba that does not come from Europe. So I rack my brain for those diamonds, like the word for okra, *quimbombo,* that vary island to island, and it is the closest I can come to fulfilling her wish.

*

We walk down the streets and children touch us. Light, like this. Pass through a sea of blue- and khaki-clad middle schoolers, surrounding us as mist, a feathery storm of inquisition and shy gazes.

*

Tonight, my friend and I take turns washing one another's hair. I lean against the concrete wall, wary of how the rotted paint flakes under my fingernails. Funk from our skin razes the air around us. I feel like a child, red dust peppered into skin, feet and legs sore, a grit that has not for days left my teeth, cheeks, hair.

The sink is a granite trough fixed to the wall that separates us from a courtyard where the woman of language is hanging clothing. She hums staccato music in Kinyarwanda, and just beyond her is the silence that deafens the countryside at night.

Her touch, competent, gentle, reminds me of being little. Of playing with my cousins in the hydrants, playing at war, then holding hands on the way back inside the apartment.

*

A man invites us to visit. As he kneads dough for bread, he points to a dark spot on the wood floor where he lay still for three days, drinking blood to stay alive, after his neighbors broke into his house and murdered his family. After the war, which was genocide, he came back home. So did his neighbors. They apologized to him, and he says he has forgiven them. I wonder what is an apology, what is forgiveness. When the bread is done we eat it with our hands. When we leave we look with fresh eyes, but we don't understand anything except the taste of the bread, which is fresh and smells perfect.

*

During the genocide, the capital city was many mass graves and roadblocks. Today it is noise, smoke rising from colored rows of shacks and open markets, people carrying yellow jugs to and from the distant water tap. The smell of the fry place where I was introduced to honey brew. A group of children roadside teasing the littlest, no older than five. She runs to me and touches my arm, then giggles and runs away. I understand it wasn't teasing but a dare. She has bright, midnight-colored eyes, and her fingers are softer than butter and rain.

I can't imagine the thick rains that fall each spring here, or the warm coin smell of blood, fluid mixed with mud. I imagine my body passing through what used to be, being what used to be, and my mind shifts open for a second, and I think I see, then it shuts blank.

*

During the prison visit, Noemi and I meet. He was ten when he took a friend's life, and then another and another, with a machete. He says, softly, matter-of-factly, *I wasn't thinking.*

We weren't thinking, explain a group of men, uttering low over each other, reaffirming one another. It is an explanation. It is not excuse.

I think about how often I stop thinking. Erase one thought to preserve another. Set up a boundary around one memory to allow another to make and then tell a story, uninterrupted.

*

Why am I here? Because here is a mirror.

The red, red earth. Trees littering flowers and so much heat. We are on a hill, facing the city. During a thunderstorm I dig my feet into the mud and hold cold beer in my mouth. I am changing. The price of changing, at least at first, is blind silence.

*

Gacaca are the community tribunals, held in town centers, logs on a bare earth for sitting, wooden railings for leaning, where people, many women, testify to harm done and witnessed. I do not understand why our group, full of white people, goes there. As if it is television. As if curiosity is relevant. It is common knowledge here that the French funded many of the tools of genocide, and white people are still suspected of being spies. I go stand far outside, separating my darker-than-white but lighter-than-Black skin from the inside place, to separate the violence of this skin into a thing I can hold and be responsible for alone. People endure and endure catastrophic violence which is unending. Unyielding. Hold to breathe. A keening builds behind my teeth. An old woman with cataract eyes is beside me. It begins to rain and it washes into the thing in my heart that is tight as a done stone, nothing to be done but say.

*

Kigali memorial: In one room, pictures clipped, hanging with no covering, curling inwards or laying flat. Skulls arranged beneath certain glass, bones arranged beneath other glass. Red pink blue clothing, mud-stained, shreds of cotton, pieced together in the outline of a bodies, also pinned behind glass. Rows of pictures of the dead when they were alive clipped together, ceiling to floor. Uncovered. When you walk through, your breath, and the trail of your body's air, parts and shakes them a little. Nobody has to tell you not to touch them.

There are long cracks in the earth, dried in drought, mirroring the mind.

There are empty rivers in the earth where our memory is supposed to be.

Coming to Bed

Night's a sea: of chanced things

like fish, nervy silver
dart in thin light,

like clouds.   — siphoning, your form loaded with stars,
                            magic of failed desire — here —

doorway
between your body and the radiator

        Climb in — thigh over thigh, so much body
        touching body that body becomes

creased lines eviscerated
by the wash of black cold

your toes curled like a
diver's   and stilled, as if broken. A sea

Tompkins Square Park

There was a fire here last night.

The pigeons are brushing ashes out of their feathers,
clucking about midnight sirens and slow-to-move firemen.

There was a fire here last night.

Women shut their windows and men locked the doors.
Children ran in stiff indoor circles, tonguing the burnt air.

There was a fire here last night.

Rilke said, *Gather honey.* The stench is

a relief, this hanging thickly. The sensible part of my brain whistles,
I hope nobody was hurt,

while the rest of me carefully folds the smoke into my hair
and hands and pockets, as if I

am enough rain to wash it away, as if I can ward off disaster
by becoming one.

Basement Trick

There are no poems left inside of me: *bitter tanning acid of grief:* how to turn words over and over until they fit together, truth, seamless as wind-parts.

Let Me Love You has come out of my mouth seventeen thousand times in the last thirty days.

Benediction: in high school I sat in a basement and a girl offered to paralyze me, and god did I want paralysis—her smooth, long white fingers tilting my head to the side, pinching down on the nerve—I said no—

Happy Ending

(After Nicanor Parra)

I.

two parallel lines
which always cut
    one other
constitute
a perfect marriage

—a river who flows against her own current stays put

silent
silent

II.

after nine months
nothing left but to abandon the premise

he sensed futility
but by that time he'd already grown

arms and feet not to mention
a taste for curried fish and so

he swam in his sheeted cave

till this one, this one, built of silence
burped him up

Love Poem X

Under it a night wind broke each lock and window.
They strained inside each other, two gun barrels quickened to fasting.

She willed her bones to earth concrete,
Excavated flesh as soil. Bit the remaindered halves.

The want to help X become free but instead became tangled in what held X which was X.
Crawl into the world's mouth thinking any warmth meant home,

especially the relics—cup of rum, singed papers and dark shining trees.

Love Poem I

When I first met X, I passed a farmer's market next to Columbia University and was overcome by the urge to cook for X. I don't know how to cook. I thought, *Oh, then this is what love is.*

Riding at Night

I left a little of the port wine on the counter for you.

Hush, baby, hush like small things hush at twilight,
where the line between us grows small.

Once I walked the narrow road between two small towns, a few miles.

I put my hands in the grass and smelled the air. This was
before I started with cigarettes.

A friend would ride that miles-long road with her bike,
in the night, no lights, terrified but flying forward.

I left something, I can't remember what, on the counter. For you,

whole worlds, astounding, rise above
sea level then collapse, equally astounding, in my chest.

Imagine that sound, the sound of worlds.
Imagine this taste, the taste of the smallest thing—

a tongue covered in the cinders of butterflies.
Yes, astonishing, how easy it is to be left.

Hush, baby, hush. Do you know how your body left a scar,
a hollow, as if I was grass,

a night to fly through. Do you know.

First Avenue Walk With Fruit

sunlight suckles
raw flap-grass
men on the corner—*precious, linda, baby, beauty, mami*—

                                        her hands are filled
                                                with voices

oh, a
tamarind—husk
        split damp fruit

                kiting away (on the tongue)

Teaching the Map

When I showed the boys a map of the world
I knew it was a bad way to teach them
The lesson—the map does not demonstrate well the bigness
Of the world. Only that Georgia is orange and that the sea is a uniform
Shade of blue. None of us have ever been to Georgia. *Why is Asia*
Cut in half? one asks. *Why do they call me African?* says
another. *Why don't the islands get drowned*
By the sea, and *where do all the names come from?* Reduced, a map is
A reduction. We are an unchecked species; we destroy
The planet with maps. *What is a border?* one asks, while another
Furtively gazes at his crush, sitting beside him, elbows
Touching unconsciously, pencils scattered like lost boats. That,
That. The swollen sting of his loving you, the quiet
In his mind that paints you distinct and shining, that is the border
We create and recreate. *New York is yellow.* The sea remains blue:
The sea is not actually blue, you know, another says. *I know*, says
Another—*it is the color of the sky. Why is the sky blue? Because space*
Is black. Black like me, says another. *Black is beautiful,* he repeats.
Galaxy children. Space children. Come to school to learn what a border is.
Come to school to cut yourself out of a thin paper of naming
Wrap yourself, perhaps find protection, not at all, or:
Confusion is its own form of uplift. Borders sometimes will separate
Us from ourselves. One more voice opens an orange with his
Fingers and the split rind fills the room. *Can I get some?* Yes—
He divides precisely, thin fingers. For once, there's enough. We go back
To the map. *It doesn't make sense about space,*
Another says. *Why if space is black is the sky blue. Is the sky even real?*
He asks. *What makes a sky a sky?* Another voice: *Land has borders but do*
Sky and sea have borders? Does blue mean
Borderless? Others shake their heads, *No*, while one says, *What if we lived without*

Borders? No we can't do that, says another. *There would be*
Too much fighting. But maybe if nobody knew who to fight we'd be forced
To get along. I like knowing where I belong, says another. *I belong*
In my home. I belong with who I love and who loves me. Another: *The*
Whole world will not love you. Another, *Haters gonna hate.* The Gulf of Mexico
Sits bright and divided. I think about the dead
Buried beneath, ghosts wandering plains, etched into the ridges and valleys
And oblivious blue of the sea. No map of the earth
Includes stars. This seems like an oversight. I am too quiet:
The boy with a crush looks at me, long and questioning. He says nothing:
I say, this is what we do, as humans, now. This is our
Way.

ACKNOWLEDGMENTS

"First Avenue Walk With Fruit" was published in the Spring 2009 Issue 3 of *No, Dear.*

A version of "House of Spirits" was published as "Havana" in the Spring 2012 issue of *Tidal Basin Review.*

A version of "Kigali Journals: 2006" was published in the Spring 2012 issue of *Tidal Basin Review.*

"Sunday Morning: Ars Poetica" was published in the 2012 Sex Issue of *Muzzle Magazine.*

"Happy Ending" was published in the 2012 Issue 8 of *PALABRA: A Magazine of Chicano & Latino Literary Art.*

"Coming to Bed" was published in the August 2013 Volume 8 of *Vinyl Poetry.*

"Visiting Your Father" was published in the May 2014 issue of *decomP magazinE.*

"Teaching The Map" was published in the Summer 2014 issue of *Five Quarterly.*

Thank You

Thank you to Marsh Hawk Press! Thank you to publisher Sandy McIntosh, who skillfully and kindly navigated this book through publication; to my editor Jon Curley, whose insight and enthusiasm brought great joy and life to our process; to Claudia Carlson, whose tremendous expertise, kindness, and collaboration gave a physical form to this writing; and to Brenda Hillman for choosing this book.

Thank you to the Jerome Foundation for funding my Travel and Study grant to Cuba in 2011. This travel allowed me to spend immersive time all over Cuba, particularly in and around Havana and Santiago, time which fueled the creation of poems in the 'Petition' sequence. The existence of these poems in their current form would not have been possible without the Foundation's generous support.

Thank you to the Teachers and Writers Collaborative for providing me a Fellowship in the 2008-2009 year that allowed me to work, in beloved community, in a small room with yellow walls and create poems to my heart's content, many of which are here.

Thank you to my excellent teachers, mentors, and poetry guides: at Brooklyn, Lou Asekoff, poetry genius of generous heart; Marjorie Welish, whose energizing and meticulous thesis conversations inspired the poems that became *these* poems; Julie Agoos, whose diligent teaching opened my mind to poetic worlds beyond those I knew to inhabit; and Lisa Jarnot, who provided the first substantive guidance to this manuscript in a small group in her living room, and whose gentle and thorough coaching prompted the completion of this book over the following years. Thank you to Ruth Foreman, to A. Van Jordan, and to Jean Valentine, extraordinary poets who provided me such gentle, clear-eyed openness and guidance.

Thank you to my poet and artist and life comrades who have touched this book and supported its evolution: Rosemary Taylor, Emilie Boone, Aricka Foreman, Kiwan Cato, Marisa Parham, Sheila Maldonado, Leidy Reyes, Roger Bonair-Agard, Eliel Lucero, Terra Holman, Mahogany Browne, Laura Swearingen-Steadwell, Natashia Underwood, Jazzy

Dendariarena, Zaqia Crawford, Sherry Hernandez, Jenny Williams, Daemond Arrindell, Bela Baez, Jeffrey Rosales, Vanessa Jimenez Gabb, George Davila, Ajani Burrell, Bruce Morrow and countless more. Forgive me for not naming you: you are here. I love you.

Thank you to my family, my constant source of support and poems. I love you.

Thank you to you tremendously beautiful young humans I have been lucky enough to meet and teach at George Jackson Academy, Bronx Prep, LEAF, Harlem RBI, and Prep for Prep. Your awakeness in the world, your desire to know yourselves and to realize your dreams, has impacted me profoundly. I realize my dream here, by making this book, in honor of your eventual realization of your own. Your daily presences in my life have been one of the biggest gifts of love I have ever been given. Go be great. Go shine.

ABOUT THE AUTHOR

Christina Olivares is the author of *Petition*, winner of YesYes Books' 2014 Vinyl 45 Chapbook Competition, and *No Map of the Earth Includes Stars*, winner of the 2014 Marsh Hawk Press Book Prize. She is a poet and educator from New York City. She earned her MFA from CUNY Brooklyn College in Poetry and her BA from Amherst College. She is the recipient of two Jerome Foundation Travel and Study Grants (2014 and 2010) and a 2008–2009 Teachers and Writers Collaborative Fellowship.

TITLES FROM MARSH HAWK PRESS

Jane Augustine, *KRAZY: Visual Poems and Performance Scripts, A Woman's Guide to Mountain Climbing, Night Lights, Arbor Vitae*

Thomas Beckett, ~~DIPSTICK~~ *(DIPTYCH)*

Sigman Byrd, *Under the Wanderer's Star*

Patricia Carlin, *Quantum Jitters, Original Green*

Claudia Carlson, *Pocket Park, The Elephant House*

Meredith Cole, *Miniatures*

Jon Curley, *Hybrid Moments*

Neil de la Flor, *An Elephant's Memory of Blizzards, Almost Dorothy*

Chard deNiord, *Sharp Golden Thorn*

Sharon Dolin, *Serious Pink*

Steve Fellner, *The Weary World Rejoices, Blind Date with Cavafy*

Thomas Fink, *Joyride, Peace Conference, Clarity and Other Poems, After Taxes, Gossip: A Book of Poems*

Norman Finkelstein, *Inside the Ghost Factory, Passing Over*

Edward Foster, *Dire Straits, The Beginning of Sorrows, What He Ought To Know, Mahrem: Things Men Should Do for Men*

Paolo Javier, *The Feeling Is Actual*

Burt Kimmelman, *Somehow*

Burt Kimmelman and Fred Caruso, *The Pond at Cape May Point*

Basil King, *The Spoken Word/the Painted Hand from Learning to Draw/A History 77 Beasts: Basil King's Bestiary, Mirage*

Martha King, *Imperfect Fit*

Phillip Lopate, *At the End of the Day: Selected Poems and An Introductory Essay*

Mary Mackey, *Travelers With No Ticket Home, Sugar Zone, Breaking the Fever*

Jason McCall, *Dear Hero,*

Sandy McIntosh, *Cemetery Chess: Selected and New Poems, Ernesta, in the Style of the Flamenco, Forty-Nine Guaranteed Ways to Escape Death, The After-Death History of My Mother, Between Earth and Sky*

Stephen Paul Miller, *There's Only One God and You're Not It, Fort Dad, The Bee Flies in May, Skinny Eighth Avenue*

Daniel Morris, *If Not for the Courage, Bryce Passage*

Sharon Olinka, *The Good City*

Christina Olivares, *No Map of the Earth Includes Stars*

Justin Petropoulos, *Eminent Domain*

Paul Pines, *Divine Madness, Last Call at the Tin Palace*

Jacquelyn Pope, *Watermark*

Karin Randolph, *Either She Was*

Rochelle Ratner, *Ben Casey Days, Balancing Acts, House and Home*

Michael Rerick, *In Ways Impossible to Fold*

Corrine Robins, *Facing It: New and Selected Poems, Today's Menu, One Thousand Years*

Eileen R. Tabios, *Sun Stigmata, The Thorn Rosary: Selected Prose Poems and New (1998–2010), The Light Sang As It Left Your Eyes: Our Autobiography, I Take Thee, English, for My Beloved, Reproductions of the Empty Flagpole*

Eileen R. Tabios and j/j hastain, *the relational elations of ORPHANED ALGEBRA*

Susan Terris, *Ghost of Yesterday, Natural Defenses*

Madeline Tiger, *Birds of Sorrow and Joy*

Harriet Zinnes, *New and Selected Poems, Weather Is Whether, Light Light or the Curvature of the Earth, Whither Nonstopping, Drawing on the Wall*

YEAR	AUTHOR	MHP POETRY PRIZE TITLE	JUDGE
2004	Jacquelyn Pope	*Watermark*	Marie Ponsot
2005	Sigman Byrd	*Under the Wanderer's Star*	Gerald Stern
2006	Steve Fellner	*Blind Date With Cavafy*	Denise Duhamel
2007	Karin Randolph	*Either She Was*	David Shapiro
2008	Michael Rerick	*In Ways Impossible to Fold*	Thylias Moss
2009	Neil de la Flor	*Almost Dorothy*	Forrest Gander
2010	Justin Petropoulos	*Eminent Domain*	Anne Waldman
2011	Meredith Cole	*Miniatures*	Alicia Ostriker
2012	Jason McCall	*Dear Hero*	Cornelius Eady
2013	Tom Beckett	~~DIPSTICK~~*(DIPTYCH)*	Charles Bernstein
2014	Christina Olivares	*No Map of the Earth Includes Stars*	Brenda Hillman

ARTISTIC ADVISORY BOARD

Toi Derricotte, Denise Duhamel, Marilyn Hacker, Allan Kornblum *(in memorium)*, Maria Mazzioti Gillan, Alicia Ostriker, Marie Ponsot, David Shapiro, Nathaniel Tarn, Anne Waldman, and John Yau.

For more information, please go to: **http://www.marshhawkpress.org.**